FIRST CAME THE INDIANS

wearing masks with crooked mouths
and noses twisted to the side.
The strange masks were the faces
of the Stone Giant
as he appeared in people's dreams.
The Iroquois believed that it was he
who had first brought sickness
into the world.
Now he helped them
to carve the masks and use his power
to make their people well.

Ojibwa

This is how you say it—o-JIB-wa.
Sometimes, they are also called
the Chippewa (CHI-puh-wa).

It was after sunset.
Birch trees shone
like pale ghosts.
Happy cries of children
came from among the trees.
Then a strange figure
moved silently
toward the children.
His face was flat and white.
It shone a little bit
in the dusk.
The children grew quiet.
Then they ran, fast,
back to their birch bark wigwams.

Probably the strange one
was one of their parents,
wearing a birch bark mask,
come to frighten them
because they had stayed out too late.
Ojibwa parents did not like
to scold their children,
so they found ways like this
to help their children to be good.
But it could have been
something else.
The children knew that
the woods and waters all around them
were full of spirits.

If someone was lost in the woods,
a forest spirit might warn him
of danger
and help him find his way home.
Still, spirits were strange
and sometimes dangerous.
Only the bravest men
would go alone to seek them out.

The beautiful white birch trees
of their forests
gave the Ojibwa
more than just their masks

and the covers for their wigwams.
Birch bark made dishes,
boxes, canoes, and even paper,
on which they wrote down songs
in picture writing.

Since the birch bark was light
and easy to carry,
the Ojibwa could move often.
Many of them lived in four different houses
during the year.
In winter they went deep into the forest
where they would be safe from storms.
In spring, they moved
near the maple trees,
to gather sap and make maple sugar.
In summer they lived
near their fields of corn.

FIRST CAME
THE INDIANS

M. J. **Wheeler**

illustrated by
James Houston

A Margaret K. McElderry Book

ATHENEUM New York *1983*

LIBRARY OF CONGRESS CATALOGING IN PUBLICATION DATA

Wheeler, Mary Jo.
First came the Indians.
"A Margaret K. McElderry book."
Summary: Describes six North American Indian tribes:
Creek, Iroquois, Chippewa, Sioux, Makah, and Hopi, detail-
ing their material culture and social structure.
1. Indians of North America—Juvenile literature.
[1. Indians of North America]   I. Houston, James A., ill.
II. Title.
E77.4.W47   1983   970.004'97   82-13916
ISBN 0-689-50258-3

Text copyright © 1983 by M.J. Wheeler
Illustrations copyright © 1983 by James Houston
Published simultaneously in Canada by McClelland & Stewart, Ltd.
Composition by Dix Type
Syracuse, New York
Printed and bound by Halliday Lithograph Company, Inc.
West Hanover, Massachusetts
First Edition

FOR TWO SARAS

4
MAKAH
NORTHWEST
COAST

3
OJIBWA

2
IROQUOIS
NORTHEAST
WOODS

5
SIOUX
GREAT
PLAINS

6
HOPI
SOUTHWEST
DESERT

1
CREEK
SOUTHEAST
WOODS

HOW THEY CAME

A long time ago
only Indians lived
in our country.
They did not call themselves
Indians.
They called themselves
by many different names.

Before they came,
only animals lived here.
The Indians came from Asia,
following the animals they hunted.
They were able to cross
into America,
for at that time the seas were
lower than they are now,
and there was more dry land.
They traveled on,
following the animals,
until they had moved
into all parts of our country.

Indians lived
in many different ways.
Some were farmers,
and some were hunters.
Some, who lived by the sea,
fished and hunted whales.
Some lived in dry places,
and some lived in rainy places.
In some places it was cold,
and in others it was hot.
Each Indian tribe had to live
in a way that would work
in the land
that was its home.

INDIANS OF THE EASTERN WOODS

In Indian times
thick, green woods
covered the eastern part
of our country.
The forest stretched all the way
from the East Coast
to the wide, brown
Mississippi River.

The Indians of the East
learned many ways to live
among the trees.
They found out how to hunt
the shy woodland animals.
They discovered which trees
gave fruit or nuts
and when to gather them.
Some of them even
cleared away enough of the forest
so that they could grow
part of the food they needed
in fields along the banks of rivers
or in clearings among the trees.

The Creek

In the land of the Creek
the forest went on and on and on.
The sun shone through the leaves.
Birds flew from tree to tree.
Paths led through the trees,
up and over green hills
and down through green valleys.
On and on they went,
joining one Creek town
with all the others far away,
through miles of forest.

Mostly, it was the men
who traveled the forest paths,
in peace or in war.
Hunters with bows and arrows
came back proudly,
carrying deer or bear
to feed their people.
While men hunted,
women worked together
in their large fields of corn.

In summer, when the first corn grew ripe,
the chief called for a messenger
to carry a bundle of sticks
to each family
who lived in one of the wooden houses
of his town.
In each house the family
kept the sticks carefully,
throwing one away each day.
When the last stick was gone,

they put out the fire in their house.
No cooking was done.
People went without eating.
The house was cleaned.
Everything old and broken
was thrown away.
When their houses were ready,
the people gathered around
the square in the center of their town.
Here, in the center,
the town's fire usually burned,
but now it, too, had been put out.
They waited,
silent,
around the empty town square.

Then runners came from the forest,
bringing four logs:
one from the north,
one from the south,
one from the east,
and one from the west.
Using these,
the chief lit a new fire
in the center of their land.
People ran with burning branches
to light the fires in their homes again.
Everyone ate the new corn.
Men danced about the death
of animals in hunts
and of enemies in wars.
Women danced of life beginning
in children and in growing corn.
People told stories and played games.
Boys and men who had been brave in war
told what they had done
and were given new names.

For the Creek,
the time of the New Corn
was the beginning
of their new year.

Iroquois

This is how you say it—IH-ruh-kwoy.

The Iroquois were not one tribe,
but five,
joined together
to help each other
in peace and in war.
They lived in villages
surrounded by high log fences
to keep out their enemies.
Iroquois houses were made of wood,
covered with thick pieces of bark.
Each house was long and narrow,
big enough for eight or ten families
to share.
The people of each longhouse
were relatives:
a woman, her sisters,
and the husbands and children
of them all.
As those children grew up,
the boys left the house,
and each one went to live
with the family of his wife.
Girls stayed on in the house
where they had been born,
and, as time passed,
they became the new head women
of their longhouse.

The women and girls of each house
worked together to grow
many kinds of
corn, beans, and squash
in their large fields.
Men often traveled far,
hunting deer in the forests,
trading with other tribes,
or fighting wars.
But in winter everyone stayed at home.
It was cold and windy then
and snow fell so fast
that it was hard to see.
Even with snowshoes
it was hard to move
through the deep snow in the woods.
Then it was good to be in the warm longhouse,
filled with friends and relatives,
with baskets of corn and dried deer meat.
Sometimes the wind did not let
the smoke get out
through the holes in the roof,
and it made tears run down people's cheeks,
but they were warm and dry
and full of laughter.

Then, if someone was sick,
drums might begin,
and men would dance in,

And in fall they camped
near lakes and streams.
Then women took birch bark canoes
and gathered the wild rice that grew on
plants in the water.
Men hunted ducks and waterbirds,
which had come to eat the rice.
And children stayed out late,
playing in the blue dusk,
among the shining birch trees.

INDIANS OF THE WEST

In Indian times
forest covered almost all
of the eastern part of the country.
But to the west,
beyond the Mississippi River,
Indians found many different kinds of land.
In the center
were the Great Plains.
Here huge herds of buffalo
roamed across the grasslands.
In the Southwest
the land was very dry,
and there were few animals to hunt.
The Northwest was almost the opposite.
Here there was so much rain
that thick forests grew.
Seals, whales, and many kinds of fish
swam along the coast.
Wherever they lived
each Indian tribe
found ways to live in its own land,
ways that were different from the ways
of Indians in all the other parts of our country.

Sioux

This is how you say it—sue.

In the land of the Sioux
there were few trees.
There were few big hills.
Mile after mile
there was nothing but grass
under the bright sky.
The wind blew through the tall grass
making patterns
like waves on the sea.
Buffalo ate the grass
and grew strong.
The sound of their feet as they ran
was like thunder.

Faster than the buffalo,
the Sioux hunters galloped
on their horses.
When the hunters had luck in their hunt,
they thanked the spirits of the buffalo.
Then the people had meat to eat.
What they could not eat
they dried in the sun.
Nothing was wasted.
They made spoons and cups from the buffalo horns.
Children made sleds from the rib bones.
The buffalo's tail was used to swat flies.

Clothes and blankets,
even their houses,
which were called tipis,
were all made of buffalo skins.
The tipis, which kept the Sioux
warm on cold winter nights
and cool on hot summer days,
were also beautiful.
Often, they were painted
with designs from dreams of spirits,
who helped the people
and showed them how to live.
Or a great warrior might paint on the tipi walls
his brave deeds:
the times he had touched an enemy
with his bare hand in battle.
and how he had silently gone
into the very center of an enemy camp
to take their horses.

The women,
who made the tipis,
could fold them up quickly
when the Sioux moved to a new place.
The tipi poles were fastened to a horse,
their back ends dragging on the ground.
Clothes, dried food, the folded tipi, buffalo skins,
babies, and old people
were all placed on top of the poles,
behind the horses, and were pulled along.

As they traveled toward
a new camping place,
hunters rode ahead,
looking for buffalo.
If they did not need to hurry,
little girls might pull their toy tipis and dolls
behind big dogs.
And boys rode their horses nearby,
looking for rabbits to shoot
with their small bows and arrows.
When they reached their new camp,
the women helped each other
to set up their tipis again.

At night, the circle of tipis glowed
from the light of the fires inside them.
People visited each other then and told stories.
Outside the camp
the only sound was the soft *shhh*
of the wind in the grass.
The only lights were the stars.

Makah

This is how you say it—muh-KAH.

The Makah lived
near the ocean.
Rain dripped from the tall,
dark trees in their forests.
The Makah used the trees
to build big houses and strong boats.
From the bark of the trees
women made raincoats and hats.
Children filled bark baskets
with berries from the forest
and shellfish from the beach.
Men came back from sea
with their boats full of fish.

Only the bravest men hunted whales.
Sometimes,
boats that had followed the whales too far
lost their way among the gray waves
and never came back.

Sometimes huge whales
crushed the boats
with their tails.
And sometimes the whale hunters were found
by the terrible killer whales,
who hunt men.

But brave men washed every day
in cold sea water
and rubbed themselves with sand.
They did this to make their bodies strong
and to win the help of the spirits.
Each one hoped that this would make him
strong enough
to kill a whale
and to become a great man
among his people.

In winter,
the days were dark
with fog and rain,
and waves crashed on the rocks.
Then the Makah sat
by the fires inside their houses.

Old people told stories
about the First Ones,
who had made each big rock,
each hill, and each river
in their land
and who had set the sun and the moon
in the sky.
Then they watched dancers,
their faces hidden by wooden masks,
dance the great dances
of the animal spirits.

Hopi

This how you say it—HO-pee.

The land of the Hopi
is almost desert.
Hills, flat on top like tables,
rise up steep
from the land below.
To the Hopi this dry and empty land
is beautiful,
and it is where they belong.
The Hopi believe
that they came here long ago
from another world
under the ground.
When they came up,
the eagle was the first
to meet them.
It was he who let them
build their homes
on the flat-topped hills
and plant corn
beside the dry riverbeds.

The Hopi have lived in this land
a long time.
Their homes are made of stone,
built to last.
Like apartments,
one family's house is built on top of another's.
From the tops of their houses
they can see far
in all directions.
When enemies were coming,

the Hopi would call everyone
into their houses.
As the last ones came in,
they would bring the ladders up with them.
Since the only doors were in the roofs
of the top apartments,
and the ladders had been taken inside,
no enemies could get in.

Eagles still fly high
over the land of the Hopi.
The eagles live far away,
as far as one can see,
in the high, snow-topped mountains.
Here, too, the Hopi believe,
live the spirits who can bring
rain to their dry land.
Hopi men make the long, hard trip
to the mountains and then climb
high among the rocks
to get eagle feathers.
They tie the feathers,
soft and white like rain clouds,
to strings or sticks.
With these, they pray for rain.
And they dance,
wearing masks decorated with eagle feathers,
to please the spirits,
so that they will bring rain
to make their corn grow
and to bless their land,
so that the people may live in peace.

INDIANS NOW

Indians were the first Americans.
Along with the plants and animals,
they lived at peace with the land.
Then the settlers came in boats,
over the ocean.
The Indians helped the first settlers learn
to live in their new country.
The settlers were new to the land.
They found it strange and wild.
They cut down the trees
and killed the animals.
The buffalo died.
The deer hid far back
in the forests.
The settlers made farms,
roads, towns, and cities.
There was no place any more
for the Indians to live
in their old ways.

Now the Indians live much like the rest of us.
Some live in cities,
and some live in the country.
Some are teachers, factory workers,
doctors.
Some are farmers, loggers,
fishermen, and sheep herders.
Many have forgotten their old ways.
But others still speak their old languages,
tell their old stories,
and dance their old dances.
It is not the same
as their old way of life.
That is gone forever.
But it is good to remember it
and to keep the parts of it
that can be kept.
Indians have been a part of our country
from the beginning.
And Indians still have much to teach us
about how to live in peace
with the land
to which we all belong.